HORSES MAKE A LANDSCAPE
LOOK MORE BEAUTIFUL

Horses Make a Landscape Look More Beautiful

P O E M S   B Y

A L I C E   W A L K E R

A Harvest/HBJ Book
HARCOURT BRACE JOVANOVICH, PUBLISHERS
San Diego   New York   London

A number of these poems were previously published in *Callaloo,*
Family Circle, Freedomways, Hurricane Alice, Ms., and *Vanity Fair.*

The lyrics quoted in "These Days" are from "Hold On John"
(John Lennon) © 1971 Northern Songs Limited. All rights
for the United States, Canada and Mexico controlled &
administered by Maclen Music, Inc. c/o Blackwood Music
Inc. under license from ATV Music. All rights reserved.
International copyright secured. Used by permission.

Library of Congress Cataloging in Publication Data
Walker, Alice, 1944–
Horses make a landscape look more beautiful.
I. Title.
PS3573.A425H6   1984   811'.54   84-6556
ISBN 0-15-642173-9   (Harvest/HBJ : pbk.)

Designed by Margaret M. Wagner
Illustration on title page by Judith Kazdym Leeds
Printed in the United States of America
First Harvest/HBJ edition 1986
F G H I J

for two who
slipped away
almost
entirely:
my "part" Cherokee
great-grandmother
Tallulah
(Grandmama Lula)
on my mother's side
about whom
only one
agreed-upon
thing
is known:
her hair was so long
she could sit on it;

and my white (Anglo-Irish?)
great-great-grandfather
on my father's side;
nameless
(Walker, perhaps?),
whose only remembered act
is that he raped
a child:
my great-great-grandmother,
who bore his son,
my great-grandfather,
when she was eleven.

Rest in peace.
The meaning of your lives
is still
unfolding.

Rest in peace.
In me
the meaning of your lives
is still
unfolding.

Rest in peace, in me.
The meaning of your lives
is still
unfolding.

Rest. In me
the meaning of your lives
is still
unfolding.

Rest. In peace
in me
the meaning
of our lives
is still
unfolding.

Rest.

Contents

We had no word for the strange animal we got from the white man—the horse. So we called it *šunka wakan*, "holy dog." For bringing us the horse we could almost forgive you for bringing us whiskey. Horses make a landscape look more beautiful.

—Lame Deer,
Lame Deer Seeker of Visions

HORSES MAKE A LANDSCAPE
LOOK MORE BEAUTIFUL

REMEMBER?

Remember me?
I am the girl
with the dark skin
whose shoes are thin
I am the girl
with rotted teeth
I am the dark
rotten-toothed girl
with the wounded eye
and the melted ear.

I am the girl
holding their babies
cooking their meals
sweeping their yards
washing their clothes
Dark and rotting
and wounded, wounded.

I would give
to the human race
only hope.

I am the woman
with the blessed
dark skin
I am the woman
with teeth repaired
I am the woman

with the healing eye
the ear that hears.

I am the woman: Dark,
repaired, healed
Listening to you.

I would give
to the human race
only hope.

I am the woman
offering two flowers
whose roots
are twin

Justice and Hope

Let us begin.

THESE MORNINGS
OF RAIN

These mornings of rain
when the house is cozy
and the phone doesn't ring
and I am alone
though snug
in my daughter's
fire-red robe

These mornings of rain
when my lover's large socks
cushion my chilly feet
and meditation
has made me one
with the pine tree
outside my door

These mornings of rain
when all noises coming
from the street
have a slippery sound
and the wind whistles
and I have had my cup
of green tea

These mornings
in Fall
when I have slept late
and dreamed
of people I like

in places where we're
obviously on vacation

These mornings
I do not need
my beloveds' arms about me
until much later
in the day.

I do not need food
I do not need the postperson
I do not need my best friend
to call me
with the latest
on the invasion of Grenada
and her life

I do not need anything.

To be warm, to be dry,
to be writing poems again
(after months of distraction
and emptiness!),
to love and be loved
in absentia
is joy enough for me.

On these blustery mornings
in a city
that could be wet
from my kisses
I need nothing else.

And then again,
I need it all.

FIRST, THEY SAID

First, they said we were savages.
But we knew how well we had treated them
and knew we were not savages.

Then, they said we were immoral.
But we knew minimal clothing
did not equal immoral.

Next, they said our race was inferior.
But we knew our mothers
and we knew that our race
was not inferior.

After that, they said we were
a backward people.
But we knew our fathers
and knew we were not backward.

So, then they said we were
obstructing Progress.
But we knew the rhythm of our days
and knew that we were not obstructing Progress.

Eventually, they said the truth is that you eat
too much and your villages take up too much
of the land. But we knew we and our children
were starving and our villages were burned
to the ground. So we knew we were not eating
too much or taking up too much of the land.

Finally, they had to agree with us.

They said: You are right. It is not your savagery
or your immorality or your racial inferiority or
your people's backwardness or your obstructing of
Progress or your appetite or your infestation of the land
that is at fault. No. What is at fault
is your existence itself.

Here is money, they said. Raise an army
among your people, and exterminate
yourselves.

In our inferior backwardness
we took the money. Raised an army
among our people.
And now, the people protected, we wait
for the next insulting words
coming out of that mouth.

LISTEN

Listen,
I never dreamed
I would learn to love you so.
You are as flawed
as my vision
As short tempered
as my breath.
Every time you say
you love me
I look for shelter.

But these matters are small.

Lying entranced
by your troubled life
within as without your arms
I am once again
Scholarly.
Studying a way
that is not mine.
Proof of evolution's
variegation.

You would choose
not to come back again,
you say.
Except perhaps
as rock or tree.

But listen, love. Though human,
that is what you are
already
to this student, absorbed.
Human tree and rock already,
to me.

S M

I tell you, Chickadee
I am afraid of people
who cannot cry
Tears left unshed
turn to poison
in the ducts
Ask the next soldier you see
enjoying a massacre
if this is not so.

People who do not cry
are victims
of soul mutilation
paid for in Marlboros
and trucks.

Resist.

Violence does not work
except for the man
who pays your salary
Who knows
if you could still weep
you would not take the job.

THE DIAMONDS ON
LIZ'S BOSOM

The diamonds on Liz's bosom
are not as bright
as his eyes
the morning they took him
to work in the mines
The rubies in Nancy's
jewel box (Oh, how he
loves red!)
not as vivid
as the despair
in his children's
frowns.

Oh, those Africans!

Everywhere you look
they're bleeding
and crying
Crying and bleeding
on some of the whitest necks
in your town.

WE ALONE

We alone can devalue gold
by not caring
if it falls or rises
in the marketplace.
Wherever there is gold
there is a chain, you know,
and if your chain
is gold
so much the worse
for you.

Feathers, shells
and sea-shaped stones
are all as rare.

This could be our revolution:
To love what is plentiful
as much as
what's scarce.

ATTENTIVENESS

When you can no longer
eat
for thinking of those
who starve
is the time to look
beneath the skin
of someone close to you.

Relative, I see the bones
shining
in your face
your hungry eye
prominent as a skull.

I see your dreams
are ashes
that attentiveness alone
does not feed you.

I have learned this winter that, yes,
I *am* afraid to die,
even if I do it gently, controlling the rage
myself.
I think of our first week here,
when we bought the rifle to use
against the men
who prowled the street
glowering at this house.
Then it seemed so logical
to shoot to kill. The heart, untroubled;
the head, quite clear of thought.
I dreamed those creatures falling stunned and bloody
across our gleaming floor,
and woke up smiling
at how natural it is
to defend one's life.

(And I will always defend my own, of course.)

But now, I think, although it is natural,
it must continue to be hard;
or "the enemy" becomes the abstraction
he is to those TV faces
we see leering over bodies
they have killed in war. The head on the stick,
the severed ears and genitals
do not conjure up
for mere killers

higher mathematics, the sound of jazz or a baby's fist;
the leer abides.

It is *those* faces, we know,
that should have died.

EVERY MORNING

Every morning I exercise
my body.
It complains
"Why are you doing this to me?"
I give it a plié
in response.
I heave my legs
off the floor
and feel my stomach muscles
rebel:
they are mutinous
there are rumblings
of dissent.

I have other things
to show,
but mostly, my body.
"Don't you see that person
staring at you?" I ask my breasts,
which are still capable
of staring back.
"If I didn't exercise
you couldn't look up
that far.
Your life would be nothing
but shoes."
"Let us at least say we're doing it
for ourselves";
my fingers are eloquent;
they never sweat.

HOW POEMS ARE MADE/A DISCREDITED VIEW

Letting go
in order to hold on
I gradually understand
how poems are made.

There is a place the fear must go.
There is a place the choice must go.
There is a place the loss must go.
The leftover love.
The love that spills out
of the too full cup
and runs and hides
its too full self
in shame.

I gradually comprehend
how poems are made.
To the upbeat flight of memories.
The flagged beats of the running
heart.

I understand how poems are made.
They are the tears
that season the smile.
The stiff-neck laughter
that crowds the throat.
The leftover love.

I know how poems are made.

There is a place the loss must go.
There is a place the gain must go.
The leftover love.

MISSISSIPPI
WINTER 1

If I had erased my life there
where the touchdown more than race
holds attention now
how martyred he would have been
his dedication to his work
how unquestionable!
But I am stoned and do not worry
—sitting in this motel room—
for when his footsteps at last disturb
the remnants of my self-pity
there will be nothing here
to point to his love of me
not even my appreciation.

MISSISSIPPI
WINTER II

When you remember me, my child,
be sure to recall that Mama was
a sinner. Her soul was lost
(according to her mama) the very
first time she questioned God. (It
weighed heavily on her, though she
did not like to tell.)
But she wanted to live and what is more
be happy
a concept not understood before the age
of twenty-one.
She was not happy
with fences.

MISSISSIPPI
WINTER III

I cradle my four-year-old daughter
in my arms
alarmed that already she smells
of Love-Is-True perfume.
A present from
her grandmother,
who loves her.
At twenty-nine my own gifts
of seduction
have been squandered. I rise
to Romance
as if it is an Occasional Test
in which my lessons of etiquette
will, thankfully, allow me to fail.

MISSISSIPPI
WINTER IV

My father and mother both
used to warn me
that "a whistling woman and a crowing
hen would surely come to
no good end." And perhaps I should
have listened to them.
But even at the time I knew
that though my end probably might
not
be good
I must whistle
like a woman undaunted
until I reached it.

LOVE IS NOT
CONCERNED

love is not concerned
with whom you pray
or where you slept
the night you ran away
from home
love is concerned
that the beating of your heart
should kill no one.

SHE SAID:

She said: "When I was with him,
I used to dream of them together.
Making love to me, he was
making love to her.
That image made me come
every time."

A woman lies alone
outside our door.
I know she dreams us
making love;
you inside me,
her lips on my breasts.

WALKER

When I no longer have your heart
I will not request your body
your presence
or even your polite conversation.
I will go away to a far country
separated from you by the sea
—on which I cannot walk—
and refrain even from sending
letters
describing my pain.

KILLERS

With their money they bought ignorance
and killed the dreamer.
But you, Chenault,* have killed
the dreamer's mother.
They tell me you smile happily
on TV,
mission "half-accomplished."

I can no longer observe such pleased mad
faces.
The mending heart breaks
to break again.

* The assassin of Martin Luther King, Jr.'s
mother, Mrs. Alberta King. His plan had been
to murder Martin Luther King, Sr., as well.

SONGLESS

What is the point
of being artists
if we cannot save our life?
That is the cry
that wakes us
in our sleep.
Being happy is not the only
happiness.
And how many gadgets
can one person manage
at one time?

Over in the Other World
the women count
their wealth
in empty
calabashes.
How to transport
food
from watering hole
to watering
hole
has ceased to be
a problem
since the animals
died
and seed grain shrunk
to fit the pocket.

Now
it is just a matter
of who can create
the finest
decorations
on the empty
pots.

They say in Nicaragua
the whole
government
writes,
makes music
and paints,
saving their own
and helping the people save
their own lives.

(I ask you to notice
who, songless,
rules us
here.)

They say in Nicaragua
the whole
government
writes
and makes
music
saving its own
and helping the people save
their own lives.

These are not containers
void of food.
These are not decorations
on empty pots.

A FEW SIRENS

Today I am at home
writing poems.
My life goes well:
only a few sirens herald disaster
in the ghetto
down the street.
In the world, people die
of hunger.
On my block we lose
jobs, housing and breasts.
But in the world
children are lost;
whole countries of children
starved to death
before the age
of five
each year;
their mothers squatted
in the filth
around the empty cooking pot
wondering:

But I cannot pretend
to know
what they wonder.
A walled horror
instead of thought
would be my mind.

And our children
gladly starve themselves.

Thinking of the food I eat
every day
I want to vomit, like
people who throw up
at will,
understanding that whether
they digest or not
they must consume.

Can you imagine?

Rather than let the hungry
inside the restaurants
Let them eat vomit, they say.
They are applauded
for this.
They are light.

But
wasn't there a time
when food was sacred?

When a dead child
starved naked
among the oranges
in the marketplace
spoiled
the appetite?

POEM AT
THIRTY-NINE

How I miss my father.
I wish he had not been
so tired
when I was
born.

Writing deposit slips and checks
I think of him.
He taught me how.
This is the form,
he must have said:
the way it is done.
I learned to see
bits of paper
as a way
to escape
the life he knew
and even in high school
had a savings
account.

He taught me
that telling the truth
did not always mean
a beating;
though many of my truths
must have grieved him
before the end.

How I miss my father!
He cooked like a person
dancing
in a yoga meditation
and craved the voluptuous
sharing
of good food.

Now I look and cook just like him:
my brain light;
tossing this and that
into the pot;
seasoning none of my life
the same way twice; happy to feed
whoever strays my way.

He would have grown
to admire
the woman I've become:
cooking, writing, chopping wood,
staring into the fire.

I SAID TO
POETRY

I said to Poetry: "I'm finished
with you."
Having to almost die
before some weird light
comes creeping through
is no fun.
"No thank you, Creation,
no muse need apply.
I'm out for good times—
at the very least,
some painless convention."

Poetry laid back
and played dead
until this morning.
I wasn't sad or anything,
only restless.

Poetry said: "You remember
the desert, and how glad you were
that you have an eye
to see it with? You remember
that, if ever so slightly?"
I said: "I didn't hear that.
Besides, it's five o'clock in the a.m.
I'm not getting up
in the dark
to talk to you."

Poetry said: "But think about the time
you saw the moon
over that small canyon
that you liked much better
than the grand one—and how surprised you were
that the moonlight was green
and you still had
one good eye
to see it with.

Think of that!"

"I'll join the church!" I said,
huffily, turning my face to the wall.
"I'll learn how to pray again!"

"Let me ask you," said Poetry.
"When you pray, what do you think
you'll see?"

Poetry had me.

"There's no paper
in this room," I said.
"And that new pen I bought
makes a funny noise."

"Bullshit," said Poetry.
"Bullshit," said I.

GRAY

I have a friend
who is turning gray,
not just her hair,
and I do not know
why this is so.

Is it a lack of vitamin E
pantothenic acid, or B-12?
Or is it from being frantic
and alone?

"How long does it take you to love someone?"
I ask her.
"A hot second," she replies.
"And how long do you love them?"
"Oh, anywhere up to several months."
"And how long does it take you
to get over loving them?"
"Three weeks," she said, "tops."

Did I mention I am also
turning gray?
It is because I *adore* this woman
who thinks of love
in this way.

OVERNIGHTS

Staying overnight in a friend's house
I miss my own bed
in San Francisco
and the man in my bed
but mostly just
my bed
It's a mattress on the floor
but so what?

This bed I'm in is lumpy
It lists to one side
It has thin covers
and is short

All night I toss and turn
dreaming of my bed
in San Francisco
with me in it
and the man too sometimes
in it
but together
Sometimes we are eating pastrami
which he likes
Sometimes we are eating
Other things

MY DAUGHTER IS COMING!

My daughter is coming!
I have bought her a bed
and a chair
a mirror, a lamp
and a desk.
Her room is all ready
except that the curtains
are torn.
Do I have time to buy shoji panels
for the window?
I do not.

First I must WRITE A SPEECH
see the doctor about my tonsils
which are dying ahead of schedule
see the barber and do a wash
cross the country
cross Brooklyn and Manhattan
MAKE A SPEECH
READ A POEM
liberate my daughter
from her father and Washington, D.C.
recross the country
and present her to her room.

My daughter is coming!

Will she like her bed,
her chair, her mirror
desk and lamp

Or will she see only
the torn curtains?

WHEN GOLDA MEIR
WAS IN AFRICA

When Golda Meir
was in Africa
she shook out her hair
and combed it
everywhere she went.

According to her autobiography
Africans loved this.

In Russia, Minneapolis, London, Washington, D.C.
Germany, Palestine, Tel Aviv and
Jerusalem
she never combed at all.
There was no point. In those
places people said, "She looks like
any other aging grandmother. She looks
like a troll. Let's sell her cookery
and guns."

"*Kreplach* your cookery," said Golda.

Only in Africa could she finally
settle down and comb her hair.
The children crept up and stroked it,
and she felt beautiful.

Such wonderful people, Africans
Childish, arrogant, self-indulgent, pompous,
cowardly and treacherous—a *great* disappointment

to Israel, of course, and really rather
ridiculous in international affairs,
but, withal, opined Golda, a people of charm
and good taste.

IF "THOSE PEOPLE"
LIKE YOU

If "those people" like you
it is a bad sign.
It is the kiss of death.
This is the kind of thing we discuss
among ourselves.

We were about to throw out
a perfectly good man.

"They are always telling me
I've got to meet him! They
are always saying how superior
he is! And those who cannot
say he's superior say 'How *Nice.*'
Well! We know what this means.
The man's insufferable. *They're*
insufferable. How can he stand
them, if he means any good to us?"

It so happened I knew this man.
"You've got to meet him," I said.
"He *is* superior, nice, and not at all
insufferable." And this is true.

But the talk continued:
If "those people" like you
it is a bad sign.
It is the kiss of death.

Because that is the kind of thing
we talk about
among ourselves.

ON SIGHT

I am so thankful I have seen
The Desert
And the creatures in The Desert
And the desert Itself.

The Desert has its own moon
Which I have seen
With my own eye

There is no flag on it.

Trees of the desert have arms
All of which are always up
That is because the moon is up
The sun is up
Also the sky
The stars
Clouds
None with flags.

If there were flags, I doubt
The trees would point.
Would you?

I'M REALLY
VERY FOND

I'm really very fond of you,
he said.

I don't like fond.
It sounds like something
you would tell a dog.

Give me love,
or nothing.

Throw your fond in a pond,
I said.

But what I felt for him
was also warm, frisky,
moist-mouthed,
eager,
and could swim away

if forced to do so.

REPRESENTING
THE UNIVERSE

There are five people in this room
who still don't know what I'm saying.
"What is she saying?" they're asking.
"What is she doing here?"

It is not enough to be interminable;
one must also be precise.

The Wasichus* did not kill them to eat; they killed them for the metal that makes them crazy, and they took only the hides to sell. Sometimes they did not even take the hides, only the tongues; and I have heard that fire-boats came down the Missouri River loaded with dried bison tongues. . . . And when there was nothing left but heaps of bones, the Wasichus came and gathered up even the bones and sold them.
                                        —Black Elk,
                                        Black Elk Speaks

* Wasichu in Sioux means "he who takes the fat."

FAMILY OF

Sometimes I feel so bad
I ask myself
Who in the world
Have I murdered?

It is a Wasichu's voice
That asks this question,
Coming from nearly inside of me.

It is asking to be let in, of course.

I am here too! he shouts,
Shaking his fist.
Pay some attention to me!

But if I let him in
What a mess he'll make!
Even now asking who
He's murdered!
Next he'll complain
Because we don't keep a maid!

He is murderous and lazy
And I fear him,
This small, white man;
Who would be neither courteous
Nor clean
Without my help.
By the hour I linger
On his deficiencies

And his unfortunate disposition,
Keeping him sulking
And kicking
At the door.

There is the mind that creates
Without loving, for instance,
The childish greed;
The boatloads and boatloads
of tongues . . .

Besides, where would he fit
If I did let him in?
No sitting at round tables
For him!

I could be a liberal
And admit one of his children;
Or be a radical and permit two.
But it is *he* asking
To be let in, alas.

Our mothers learned to receive him occasionally,
Passing as Christ. But this did not help us much.
Or perhaps it made all the difference.

But there. He is bewildered
And tuckered out with the waiting.
He's giving up and going away.
Until the next time.

And murdered quite sufficiently, too, I think,
Until the next time.

EACH ONE, PULL ONE
(Thinking of Lorraine Hansberry)

We must say it all, and as clearly
as we can. For, even before we are dead,
they are busy
trying to bury us.

Were we black? Were we women? Were we gay?
Were we the wrong *shade* of black? Were we yellow?
Did we, God forbid, love the wrong person, country
or politics? Were we Agnes Smedley or John Brown?

But, most of all, did we write exactly what we saw,
as clearly as we could? Were we unsophisticated
enough to cry *and* scream?

Well, then, they will fill our eyes,
our ears, our noses and our mouths
with the mud
of oblivion. They will chew up
our fingers in the night. They will pick
their teeth with our pens. They will sabotage
both our children
and our art.

Because when we show what we see,
they will discern the inevitable:
We do not worship them.

We do not worship them.
We do not worship what they have made.
We do not trust them.

We do not believe what they say.
We do not love their efficiency.
Or their power plants.
We do not love their factories.
Or their smog.
We do not love their television programs.
Or their radioactive leaks.
We find their papers boring.
We do not worship their cars.
We do not worship their blondes.
We do not envy their penises.
We do not think much
of their Renaissance.
We are indifferent to England.
We have grave doubts about their brains.

In short, we who write, paint, sculpt, dance
or sing
share the intelligence and thus the fate
of all our people
in this land.
We are not different from them,
neither above nor below,
outside nor inside.
We are the same.
And we do not worship them.

We do not worship them.
We do not worship their movies.
We do not worship their songs.
We do not think their newscasts
cast the news.
We do not admire their president.
We know why the White House is white.

We do not find their children irresistible;
We do not agree they should inherit the earth.

But lately you have begun to help them
bury us. You who said: King was just a womanizer;
Malcom, just a thug; Sojourner, folksy; Hansberry,
a traitor (or whore, depending); Fannie Lou Hamer,
merely spunky; Zora Hurston, Nella Larsen, Toomer:
reactionary, brainwashed, spoiled by whitefolks, minor;
Agnes Smedley, a spy.

I look into your eyes;
you are throwing in the dirt.
You, standing in the grave
with me. Stop it!

Each one must pull one.

Look, I, temporarily on the rim
of the grave,
have grasped my mother's hand
my father's leg.
There is the hand of Robeson
Langston's thigh
Zora's arm and hair
your grandfather's lifted chin
the lynched woman's elbow
what you've tried to forget
of your grandmother's frown.

Each one, pull one back into the sun

We who have stood over
so many graves
know that no matter what *they* do
all of us must live
or none.

WHO?

Who has not been
invaded
by the Wasichu?

Not I, said the people.

Not I, said the trees.

Not I, said the waters.

Not I, said the rocks.

Not I, said the air.

Moon!

We hoped
you were safe.

WITHOUT
COMMERCIALS

Listen,
stop tanning yourself
and talking about
fishbelly
white.
The color white
is not bad at all.
There are white mornings
that bring us days.
Or, if you must,
tan only because
it makes you happy
to be brown,
to be able to see
for a summer
the whole world's
darker
face
reflected
in your own.

*

Stop unfolding
your eyes.
Your eyes are
beautiful.
Sometimes
seeing you in the street
the fold zany
and unexpected

I want to kiss
them
and usually
it is only
old
gorgeous
black people's eyes
I want
to kiss.

       **

Stop trimming
your nose.
When you
diminish
your nose
your songs
become little
tinny, muted
and snub.
Better you should
have a nose
impertinent
as a flower,
sensitive
as a root;
wise, elegant,
serious and deep.
A nose that
sniffs
the essence
of Earth. And knows

the message
of every
leaf.

***

Stop bleaching
your skin
and talking
about
so much black
is not beautiful
The color black
is not bad
at all.
There are black nights
that rock
us
in dreams.
Or, if you must,
bleach only
because it pleases you
to be brown,
to be able to see
for as long
as you can bear it
the whole world's
lighter face
reflected
in your own.

****

As for me,
I have learned
to worship
the sun
again.
To affirm
the adventures
of hair.

For we are all
splendid
descendants
of Wilderness,
Eden:
needing only
to see
each other
without
commercials
to believe.

Copied skillfully
as Adam.

Original

as Eve.

NO ONE CAN WATCH THE WASICHU

No one can watch
the Wasichu
anymore
He is always
penetrating
a people
whose country
is too small
for him
His bazooka
always
sticking up
from some
howling
mother's
backyard.

No one can watch
the Wasichu
anymore
He is always
squashing
something
Somebody's guts
trailing
his shoe.

No one can watch
the Wasichu
anymore

He is scalping
the earth
till she runs
into the ocean
The dust of her
flight
searing
our sight.

No one can watch
the Wasichu
anymore
Smirking
into our bedrooms
with his
terrible
Nightly News . . .

No one can watch
the Wasichu
anymore.

Regardless.

He has filled
our every face
with his window.

Our every window
with
his face.

THE THING ITSELF

Now I am going
to rape you,
you joked;
after a pleasure
wrung
from me.

With playful roughness
you dragged my body
to meet yours;
on your face
the look of
mock
lust
you think
all real women
like

As all "real" women
really
like rape.

Lying
barely breathing
beneath
your heaving
heaviness
I fancied I saw
my great-great-grandmother's
small hands

encircle
your pale neck.

There was no
pornography
in her world
from which to learn
to relish the pain.

(She was the thing
itself.)

Oh, you who seemed
the best of them,
my own sad
Wasichu;
in what gibberish
was our freedom
engraved on
our chains.

TORTURE

When they torture your mother
plant a tree
When they torture your father
plant a tree
When they torture your brother
and your sister
plant a tree
When they assassinate
your leaders
and lovers
plant a tree
When they torture you
too bad
to talk
plant a tree.

When they begin to torture
the trees
and cut down the forest
they have made
start another.

WELL.

Well.

He was a poet
a priest
a revolutionary
compañero
and we were right
to be seduced.

He brought us greetings
from his countrypeople
and informed us
with lifted
fist
that they would not
be moved.

All his poems
were eloquent.

I liked
especially
the one
that said
the revolution
must
liberate
the cougars, the trees,
and the lakes;
when he read it

everyone
breathed
relief;
ecology
lives
of all places
in Central
America!
we thought.

And then he read
a poem
about Grenada
and we
smiled
until he began
to describe
the women:

Well. One woman
when she smiled
had shiny black
lips
which reminded him
of black legs
(vaselined, no doubt),
her whole mouth
to the poet
revolutionary
suddenly
a leg
(and one said
What?)

Another one,
duly noted by
the priest,
apparently
barely attentive
at a political
rally
eating
a mango

Another wears
a red dress,
her breasts
(no kidding!)
like coconuts. . . .

Well. Nobody ever said
supporting other people's revolutions
wouldn't make us
ill:

But what a pity
that
the poet
the priest
and the revolution
never seem
to arrive
for the black woman,
herself.

Only for her black lips
or her black leg
does one or the other

arrive;
only for her
devouring mouth
always depicted
in the act
of eating
something colorful

only for her breasts
like coconuts
and her red dress.

SONG

The world is full of colored
people
People of Color
Tra-la-la
The world is full of
colored people
Tra-la-la-la-la.

They have black hair
and black and brown
eyes
The world is full of
colored people
Tra-la-la.

The world is full of colored
people
People of Color
Tra-la-la
The world is full of colored
people
Tra-la-la-la-la.

Their skins are pink and yellow
and brown
All colored people
People of Color
Colored people
Tra-la-la.

Some have full lips
Some have thin
Full of colored people
People of Color
Colored lips
Tra-la-la.

The world is full of
colored people
People of Color
Colorful people
Tra-la-la!

THESE DAYS

Some words for people I think of as friends.

These days I think of Belvie
swimming happily in the country pond
coating her face with its mud.
She says:
"We could put the whole bottom of this pond in jars
and sell it to the folks
in the city!"
Lying in the sun she dreams
of making our fortune, à la Helena Rubenstein.
Bottling the murky water
too smelly to drink,
offering exotic mud facials and mineral baths
at exorbitant fees.
But mostly she lies in the sun
dreaming of water, sun and the earth
itself—

Surely the earth can be saved for Belvie.

These days I think of Robert
folding his child's tiny shirts
consuming TV dinners ("A kind of *processed* flavor")
rushing off each morning to school—then to the office,
the supermarket, the inevitable meeting: writing,
speaking, marching against oppression, hunger,
ignorance.
And in between having a love affair
with tiny wildflowers and gigantic
rocks.

"Look at this one!" he cries,
as a small purple face
raises its blue eye to the sun.
"Wow, look at that one!" he says,
as we pass a large rock
reclining beside the road.
He is the man with child
the new old man.
Brushing hair, checking hands, nails
and teeth.
A sick child finds comfort
lying on his chest all night
as do I.

Surely the earth can be saved for Robert.

These days I think of Elena.
In the summers, for years, she camps
beside the Northern rivers
sometimes with her children
sometimes with women friends
from "way, way back."
She is never too busy to *want* at least
to join a demonstration
or to long to sit
beside
a river.
"I will not think less of you
if you do *not* attend this meeting," she says,
making us compañeras for life.

Surely the earth can be saved for Elena.

These days I think of Susan;
so many of her people lost
in the Holocaust. Every time I see her
I can't believe it.
"You have to have some of my cosmos seeds!"
she says
over the phone. "The blooms
are glorious!"
Whenever we are together
we eat a lot.
If I am at her house
it is bacon, boiled potatoes,
coffee and broiled fish:
if she is at my house it is
oyster stew, clams, artichokes
and wine.
Our dream is for time in which
to walk miles together, a couple
of weeds stuck between our teeth,
comfy in our yogi pants
discoursing on Woolf
and child raising,
essay writing and gardening.
Susan makes me happy
because she exists.

Surely the earth can be saved for Susan.

These days I think of Sheila.
" 'Sheila' is already a spiritual name," she says.
And "Try meditation and jogging both."
When we are together we talk
and talk

about The Spirit.
About What is Good and What is Not.
There was a time she applauded my anger,
now she feels it is something I should outgrow.
"It is not a useful emotion," she says. "And besides,
if you think about it, there's nothing worth
getting angry about."
"I do not like anger," I say.
"It raises my blood pressure.
I do not like violence. So much has been done to me.
But having embraced my complete being
I find anger
and the capacity for violence
within me.
Control
rather than eradication
is about the best
I feel I can do.
Besides, they intend to murder us,
you know."
"Yes, I understand," she says.
"But try meditation
and jogging *both*;
you'll be surprised how calm you feel."
I meditate, walk briskly, and take deep, deep breaths
for I know the importance of peace to the inner self.
When I talk to Sheila
I am forced to honor
my own ideals.

Surely the earth can be saved for Sheila.

These days I think of Gloria.
"The mere *sight* of an airplane puts me to sleep,"
she says.
Since she is not the pilot, this makes sense.
If this were a courageous country,
it would ask Gloria to lead it
since she is sane and funny and beautiful and smart
and the National Leaders we've always had
are not.
When I listen to her talk about women's rights
children's rights
men's rights
I think of the long line of Americans
who should have been president, but weren't.
Imagine Crazy Horse as president. Sojourner Truth.
John Brown. Harriet Tubman. Black Elk or Geronimo.
Imagine President Martin Luther King confronting
the youthful "Oppie" Oppenheimer. Imagine President
Malcolm X going after the Klan. Imagine President Stevie
Wonder dealing with the "Truly Needy."
Imagine President Shirley Chisholm, Ron Dellums or
Sweet Honey in the Rock
dealing with Anything.
It is imagining to make us weep with frustration,
as we languish under real estate dealers, killers,
and bad actors.

Gloria makes me aware of how much we lose by denying,
exiling or repressing parts of ourselves
so that other parts,
grotesque and finally lethal
may creep into the light.

"Women must seize the sources of reproduction," she says,
knowing her Marx and her Sanger too.

Surely the earth can be saved for Gloria.

These days I think of Jan,
who makes the most exquisite goblets
—and plates and casseroles.
Her warm hands steady on the cool
and lively clay,
her body attentive and sure, bending over the wheel.
I could watch her work for hours—
but there is never time. On one visit I see the bags
of clay. The next visit, I see pale and dusty molds,
odd pieces of hardening handles and lids. On another,
I see a stacked kiln. On another, magical objects of use
splashed with blue, streaked with black and red.
She sits quietly beside her creations
at countless fairs
watching without nostalgia
their journeys into the world.
She makes me consider how long
people have been making things. How wise
and thoughtful people often are.
A world without Jan would be like her house
when she is someplace else—gray, and full of furniture
I've never seen before.

Our dream is to sit on a ridge top for days
and reminisce
about the anti-nuke movement.
The time we were together

at a women's music festival, and Diablo Canyon
called her.
The more comic aspects
of her arrest.

There is a way that she says "um *hum*" that means a lot
to me.

Surely the earth can be saved for Jan.

These days I think of Rebecca.
"Mama, are you a racist?" she asks.
And I realize I have badmouthed white people
once too often
in her presence.

Years ago I would have wondered
how white people have managed to live
all these years
with this question
from their children;
or, how did they train their children
not to ask?

Now I think how anti-racism
like civil rights or
affirmative action
helps white people too.
Even if they are killing us
we have to say, to try to believe,
it is the way they are raised,
not genetics,
that causes their bizarre,

death-worshiping
behavior.

"If we were raised like white people,
to think we are superior to everything else
God made, we too would behave the way
they do," say the elders.
And: "White folks could *be* people of color
if they'd only relax."

Besides, my daughter declares
her own white father "Good," and reminds me
it is often black men
who menace us on
the street.

Talking to Rebecca about race almost always
guarantees a headache.
But that is a small price
for the insight and clarity
she brings.

Surely the earth can be saved for Rebecca.

These days I think of John, Yoko and Sean Lennon.
Whenever I listen
to "Working-Class Hero,"
I laugh: because John says "fucking"
twice,
and it is always a surprise
though I know the record by heart.
I like to imagine
him putting Sean to bed

or exchanging his own hard,
ass-kicking boots
for sneakers.
I like to imagine Yoko
making this white boy deal with the word NO
for the first time.
And the word YES forever.
I like to think of this brave
and honest
new age family
that dared to sing itself
even as anger, fear, sadness and death
squeezed its vocal cords.

Yoko knows the sounds of a woman coming
are finer by far than those of a B-52
on a bombing raid.

And a Kotex plastered across
a man's forehead at dinner
can indicate serenity.

> *Hold on world*
> *World hold on*
> *It's gonna be all right*
> *You gonna see the light*
> *(Ohh) when you're one*
> *Really one*
> *You get things done*
> *Like they never been done*
> *So hold on.**

* From "Hold On John" by John Lennon.

Surely the earth can be saved
by all the people
who insist
on love.

Surely the earth can be saved for us.